Miraculous Magic Tricks

MIND MAGIC

by Mike Lane

Illustrations by David Mostyn

WINDMILL
BOOKS ™

New York

Published in 2012 by Windmill Books, an Imprint of Rosen Publishing
29 East 21st Street, New York, NY 10010

First Edition

Author: Mike Lane
Editors: Patience Coster and Joe Harris
Illustrations: David Mostyn
Design: Tokiko Morishima

Library of Congress Cataloging-in-Publication Data

Lane, Mike.
 Mind magic / by Mike Lane.
    p. cm. — (Miraculous magic tricks)
 Includes index.
 ISBN 978-1-61533-514-5 (library binding) —
ISBN 978-1-4488-6735-6 (pbk.) —
ISBN 978-1-4488-6736-3 (6-pack)
1. Magic tricks—Juvenile literature. 2. Telepathy—
Juvenile literature. I. Title.
 GV1553.L36 2012
 793.8—dc23
                        2011028921

Printed in China

CPSIA Compliance Information: Batch # AW2102WM: For further information
contact Windmill Books, New York, New York at 1-866-478-0556

CONTENTS

INTRODUCTION

Within these pages you will discover great mind magic tricks that are easy to do and impressive to watch.

To be a successful magician, you will need to practice the tricks in private before you perform them in front of an audience. An excellent way to practice is in front of a mirror, since you can watch the magic happen before your own eyes.

When performing, you must speak clearly, slowly, and loudly enough for everyone to hear. But never tell the audience what's going to happen.

Remember to "watch your angles." This means being careful about where your spectators are standing or sitting when you are performing. The best place is directly in front of you.

Never tell the secret of how the trick is done. If someone asks, just say: "It's magic!"

THE MAGICIAN'S PLEDGE

I promise not to reveal the secrets of magic to those who are not magicians.

I promise to practice these magic tricks over and over again before attempting to perform them in front of an audience.

I promise to respect my art, the art of magic.

THE MIND'S EYE

1 Prior to the trick, the magician cuts a small square window in the bottom right-hand corner of a card box. The window should be just big enough to show the card value from the corner of the card. It should be on the side of the box where the flap slots in.

2 The magician holds up the box of cards and shows the audience both sides. When showing the side with the window, the magician covers it with his thumb.

3 The magician takes the deck from the box and asks a spectator to shuffle it.

4 The magician places the deck back in the box, with the faces of the cards toward the secret window.

5 The magician lifts the pack of cards to his forehead, ensuring that the window is facing him. As he does this, he twists the box upright and peeks at the card in the window.

6 The magician closes his eyes and concentrates. He explains that he will see the first card in the deck in his mind's eye. He then names the card.

7 He opens the box, removes the card, and shows it to the spectator. The next card will now be visible through the window. The trick can be repeated as often as the magician likes.

PICK IT PREDICTION

ILLUSION

The magician names several cards and asks different spectators to pick any card from a face-down deck. They turn out to be the cards the magician predicted the spectators would choose.

1 The magician spreads out a deck of cards face down in front of the spectators. The magician should have looked at and memorized the bottom card.

2 The magician says to the first spectator: "I make a prediction that you will pick…" —and names the bottom card. He then asks the spectator to point to a card.

3 The magician picks up the card the spectator pointed to, looks at it, and says, "Very good."

9

4 He does not show the card to the spectator, but puts it to one side, face down.

5 The magician now says to the second spectator: "I make a prediction that you will pick…" —and names the card the first spectator picked. He asks the second spectator to point to a card.

6 The magician picks it up, looks at it, and says, "Excellent."

7 He puts the card aside, face down, with the other card.

8 The magician says to the third spectator: "I make a prediction that you will pick…" —and names the card the second spectator picked. He asks the third spectator to point to a card. The magician picks it up, looks at it, says, "You three are great at this," and puts it aside with the others.

9 The magician now states that he will also pick a card. He names the card the third spectator chose, picks up the bottom card, and puts it aside with the others.

10 The magician now shows all four cards to the spectators. They are the four cards the magician predicted would be picked.

PHANTOM TOUCH

1 The magician chooses a spectator and asks him or her to stand directly in front of him.

2 The magician extends his two index fingers, curling the rest of his fingers into fists.

3 Keeping his hands together, he holds them out in front of himself at eye level. The magician says he will touch the spectator's forehead with his index fingers.

4 The magician slowly moves his fingers toward the spectator's forehead, telling the spectator to keep his eyes closed tight or the experiment won't work.

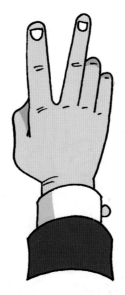

5 Once the spectator's eyes are closed, the magician extends his middle finger on one hand to form a "V" with the index finger. He touches the spectator's forehead with these fingers.

6 As he touches the spectator's forehead with one hand, the magician quickly taps the spectator's shoulder with his other hand.

7 The magician now immediately places his hands together in front of himself in the position the spectator last saw them in. He tells the spectator to open his eyes and asks if he felt the phantom touch.

MR. MAGUS

ILLUSION

The magician asks a spectator to name any playing card. The magician calls Mr. Magus on the phone and Mr. Magus tells the spectator the card he named.

1 Prior to the trick, the magician asks a friend to play the part of Mr. Magus. The magician and Mr. Magus will need to rehearse this trick many times over the phone before attempting to do it in front of an audience.

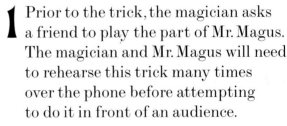

2 To perform the trick, the magician asks the spectator to name any playing card.

3 The magician says that he will call Mr. Magus, and picks up the phone.

HELLO, MAY I SPEAK TO MR. MAGUS?

ACE, 2, 3, 4, 5, 6, 7...

HELLO, MR. MAGUS

4 When his friend answers the phone, the magician starts the following sequence: Magician: "Hello, may I speak to Mr. Magus?" Mr. Magus, counting slowly: "Ace, 2, 3, 4, 5, 6, 7, 8, 9, 10, Jack, Queen, King."

5 When Mr. Magus reaches the value of the spectator's card, the magician says: "Hello, Mr. Magus."

CLUB, DIAMOND, HEART...

HOLD ON, PLEASE.

6 Mr. Magus now slowly says the suits: "Club, Diamond, Heart, Spade." When the friend names the right suit, the magician once again stops him by saying, "Hold on, please." Now the friend knows the card value and the suit.

7 OF HEARTS.

7 The magician hands the phone to the spectator and tells her to ask Mr. Magus what her card is. In his best "Mr. Magus" voice, the friend identifies the spectator's card.

A MIRROR IMAGE

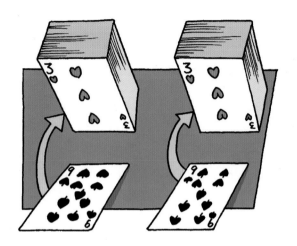

ILLUSION

The magician and spectator each have a deck of cards. They split their decks and the top and bottom cards turn out to be the same in each deck.

1 Prior to the trick, the magician prepares the decks. He places the same card on the bottom of each deck. Now he places another two cards, also the same, under the bottom cards. The second pair of cards should face upward so that they are face to face with the third from bottom card. The magician must not allow the spectator to see the bottom card.

2 To perform the trick, the magician places both decks on a table and asks the spectator to choose one and hold it behind her back. The magician does the same with the other deck.

3 The magician asks the spectator to take the top half of her deck and place it face up under the bottom half. She should do this behind her back. The magician does the same with his deck.

4 Both decks are placed on the table once more. The magician asks the spectator to find the place in the deck where the two halves meet. He asks the spectator to do the same with the other deck.

5 The cards where the two halves meet are the same in both decks. A mirror image!

FRACTION CARD

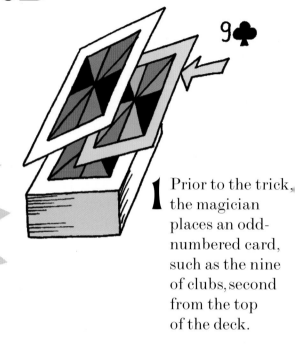

ILLUSION

The magician asks the spectator to choose a card from a deck. He then asks the spectator to divide the number of that card in half. The magician has a sealed envelope with a prediction card inside. The spectator opens the envelope and discovers that the card inside correctly predicts the figure he thought of.

1 Prior to the trick, the magician places an odd-numbered card, such as the nine of clubs, second from the top of the deck.

2 The magician divides the number in half. In this case, the answer is 4½. The magician takes the four of clubs out of the deck.

3 He writes the ½ fraction next to both number fours on the card.

4 He also draws a ½ club in the middle of the card. He places the card in an envelope.

5 To perform the trick, the magician takes the deck and cuts it in half.

6 He takes the top card from the top half of the deck and places it on the bottom half of the deck.

7 He points to the new top card of the top half (in this case, the nine of clubs) and asks the spectator to take that card and hold on to it.

8 The magician asks the spectator to look at the card she is holding and divide the number in half. He tells the spectator that Jacks have a value of 11, Queens have a value of 12, and Kings have a value of 13. This is a red herring, of course, because the magician already knows what the card is. The spectator may ask what to do if it is an odd-numbered card. The magician says: "It doesn't matter – whatever the card is, just divide it in half."

9 The magician hands the envelope to the spectator, who opens it and finds the fraction card.

THIS IS IT!

ILLUSION

While the magician is outside the room, a spectator touches one of ten cards. When the magician returns, he is able to tell the spectator which card he touched.

1 The magician will need an assistant for this trick. The magician places ten cards on a table. The cards should be positioned the same way as the pips (Hearts, Spades, Clubs, or Diamonds) are on a playing card with the value of ten. This is called the line-up. The magician must ensure that there is a ten card in the line-up. The cards should be face up.

2 The magician tells a spectator to touch one card while he is out of the room and allow the other spectators to see which card he touches.

3 When the magician returns, the assistant, who has seen the card that was touched, must now work with the magician. The assistant touches each card, starting from the top of one side. Each time he touches a card, he says: "This could be it."

4 When the assistant reaches the ten card, he must touch the pip on the card that corresponds to the location of the touched card in the line-up. The magician waits until the assistant has finished with all the cards.

5 The magician concentrates and places his hand over each card as if feeling the energy. But he already knows the location of the touched card because the assistant has shown it to him.

6 The magician now returns to the spectator's card and others near it and feels around them. He finally settles on the spectator's card, declaring: "This is it!"

NUMBER CRUNCH

ILLUSION

The magician asks the spectator to write down any three-digit number of his choice. After a bit of subtraction and addition, the magician says the answer is 1089, and indeed it is.

MAGIC TIP!
REMEMBER, IT'S REVERSE-SUBTRACT-REVERSE-ADD!

1 This is a mathematical magic trick. The spectator is asked to write down any three-digit number, making sure that all three digits are different and with no zeros—for example, 568.

2a The magician asks the spectator to reverse that number and subtract the smaller number from the larger one, for example, 865 – 568 = 297. (If the difference is two digits, the spectator must use a zero in front of the number. For example, the number 99 becomes 099.)

865 – 568 = 297

2b The magician now asks the spectator to reverse this new number. So, in our example, 297 becomes 792.

297 ⟶ 792

792 + 297 = 1089

2c He then asks the spectator to add this to the number before it was reversed, for example, 792 + 297.

3 The answer will always be 1089.

1-2-3-4

ILLUSION
The magician can tell which number or card a spectator is thinking of.

1 Write down, or print out, the numbers 1 2 3 4 on a sheet of paper. They should all be the same size.

2 Hand the sheet to a spectator and tell him to think of one of the numbers.

MAGIC FACT!
REMEMBER, THIS TRICK IS BASED ON STATISTICS. IT DOES NOT ALWAYS WORK AND THEREFORE IT IS MORE OF A FUN TRICK THAN A MAGIC TRICK!

3 Take the sheet back and look at the numbers as if studying them. Announce that the number he was thinking of was 3. There is no particular explanation as to why this often works, but most people pick 3! This trick can also be done with cards. Place four playing cards directly in front of the spectator and ask him to think of one of the cards. It will usually be the third card.

THE CHOSEN ONE

ILLUSION

The magician says he will leave the room and asks a spectator to name any item in the room in his absence. When he returns, the magician can tell what item has been named.

1 The magician needs an assistant for this trick. The magician picks a spectator from the audience. He says that while he is outside the room, the spectator should name any item he can see. The assistant stays in the room.

2 Let's say the spectator names the TV as his chosen item.

MAGIC TIP!
YOU CAN PERFORM THIS TRICK SEVERAL TIMES FOR AN AUDIENCE. IF THE SPECTATORS THINK THEY HAVE WORKED OUT THE TRICK, PERFORM IT AGAIN TO SHOW THEM THAT THEY ARE WRONG!

3 Once the spectator has named the item, the assistant asks the magician to return.

4 The assistant starts naming the items in the room, as follows: "Is it the lamp? Is it the refrigerator? Is it the chair? Is it the TV? Is it the book… ?"

5 The magician waits until the assistant has finished and says: "It's the TV." The magician knows this because he has already agreed a code with his assistant. The chosen item is the one named after the item with four legs (in this case, the chair).

6 Often the spectators believe that the trick depends on the number of items that the assistant says before naming the right object. The assistant should vary where the correct item is in the list.

FURTHER READING

Barnhart, Norm. *Amazing Magic Tricks.* Mankato, MN: Capstone Press, 2008.

Cassidy, John and Michael Stroud. *Klutz Book of Magic.* Palo Alto, CA: Klutz Press, 2006.

Klingel, Cynthia. *Magic Tricks.* Mankato, MN: Compass Point Books, 2002.

Longe, Bob. *Classic Magic Tricks.* New York, NY: Metro Books, 2002.

Tremaine, Jon. *Instant Magic.* Hauppauge, NY: Barron's Educational Series, 2009.

GLOSSARY

mirror image (MIR-ur IH-mij) Something that looks just like something else.

phantom (FAN-tum) Something that seems to be there but is not real; a ghost.

predict (prih-DIKT) To make a guess based on facts or knowledge.

spectator (SPEK-tay-ter) A person who sees or watches something.

subtraction (sub-TRAK-shun) When one number is taken away from another.

WEB SITES

For Web resources related to the subject of this book, go to: www.windmillbooks.com/weblinks and select this book's title.

INDEX